The Little Book of Natural
Wonders Series

A LITTLE BOOK OF HUMMINGBIRDS

LITTLE BOOKS OF FLOWERS:

DAHLIAS / PEONIES / TULIPS

A Little Book of
Hummingbirds

Tara Austen Weaver

Illustrations by Emily Poole

SASQUATCH BOOKS | SEATTLE

For my mother, my original hummingbird, with all my love.

If there are more extraordinary birds than hummingbirds—those exotic creatives the Brazilians call *beija-flores*, flower-kissers—it is difficult to imagine what they might be.

—RONALD ORENSTEIN

Contents

Origin of the Species 8

How a Hummingbird Works 28

Selected Species 40

Creating a Hummingbird
Haven 102

Bird-watching 122

Glossary 137
Resources 140

Origin of the Species

A flash of harmless lightning,
a mist of rainbow dyes.
The burnished sunbeams
    brightening.
From flower to flower he flies.

—JOHN BANISTER TABB

The smallest known hummingbird is the Bee hummingbird of Cuba, which weigh *less than a dime; the largest is the Giant hummingbird, found in the Andes.*

It's that flicker of glinting color—sometimes no more than a tiny rapid wingbeat disturbing the air—that tells us a hummingbird is nearby. These iridescent wonders delight all those lucky enough to view them. From the smallest Bee hummingbird of Cuba, weighing in at less than 2 grams, to the Giant hummingbird of the Andes, which weighs ten times as much, these small, colorful birds have captured our attention like few others. It's no surprise that Spanish explorers, the first Europeans we know of to see these very American birds, referred to them as *joyas voladoras*—flying jewels.

Hummingbirds are a contradiction. How can such small, delicate creatures migrate from Mexico to Alaska? They have the fastest metabolic rate of any warm-blooded animal but can slow down their system to enter a type of hibernation when needed. Their wings move not up and down, but in figure eights, enabling them to navigate in any direction.

Found only in the Americas, the history of hummingbirds is not fully known—their small, hollow bones decompose too quickly to have left a significant collection of fossils. One of the few known fossil specimens was discovered in 1994 in southeastern Germany, giving rise to theories that hummingbirds originated in Eurasia, migrated to the Americas, then died off in their native lands. Scientists estimate that hummingbirds split from the swifts, their closest avian relations, about 42 million years ago.

Hummingbirds may not have much of a fossil history, but there is a rich cultural history to these fascinating birds. They play a role in oral traditions, folklore, and crafts throughout the Americas.

The Hopi and Zuni people of the southwestern United States credit the hummingbird with bringing much-needed rain from the gods to the people. A traditional tale from Puerto Rico tells the story of a boy and a girl who fall in love. Because their rival tribes do not approve of the union, the girl transforms herself into a red flower who is visited regularly by the boy, now in the form of a hummingbird. In Northern California, the Ohlone tell the story of how the hummingbird stole fire from the badgers and gave it to the people. The red-feathered throat of the hummingbird is due to a piece of coal that fell and permanently marked the bird with the color of flames. These are just a few examples of numerous hummingbird origin stories.

Though small in stature, hummingbirds were known as symbols of strength in cultures throughout the Americas. In southern Peru, the Nazca people etched a massive hummingbird figure into the red desert. Dating as far back as 200 BC, the figure is over a thousand feet long—about equal to the height of the Empire State

Building in New York. Some of the figures that the Nazca drew are so large and can only be fully seen from the air. As a result, the designs did not become apparent to modern humans until the adoption of air travel in the 1920s. The significance of these giant figures is unclear, but anthropologists assume some spiritual connection due to the existence of nearby grave sites.

Starting in the early 1300s, the Mexica people in what is now southern Mexico worshipped the Aztec god Huitzilopochtli, who was known as the Left-handed Hummingbird; it was said that fallen warriors in his army would be transformed into hummingbirds. The Taino people of the Caribbean, who believed hummingbirds were symbols of rebirth, called their young men Hummingbird Warriors. This, unfortunately, did not protect them from the violence brought in 1492 by Christopher Columbus and other European explorers, who wiped out as many as three million Taino by the early 1500s. These European explorers also brought news of the hummingbird back to Europe, spreading their popularity but endangering their numbers.

European thirst for empire was on the rise, and a number of curios were being brought back from far corners of the globe to fill "curiosity cabinets" being assembled by scientists and aristocrats across the continent. One such collector was John Gould, who became the most celebrated ornithologist and bird artist of Victorian-era Britain. He helped Charles Darwin develop his theory of natural selection (Gould's work on finches is referenced in *On the Origin of Species*, Darwin's seminal work on evolutionary biology). Gould was also a great fancier of hummingbirds.

Gould's hummingbird collection was vast—more than three hundred species. This assembly allowed him to complete what is considered his masterpiece: *A Monograph of the Trochilidae, or Family of Humming-birds*, the first volume published in 1849. Twelve years in the making, the monograph includes 360 illustration plates, many decorated with gold and silver leaf to evoke the shimmering nature of hummingbird feathers.

Gould played a big part in popularizing the humming-bird in Europe. His collection was exhibited in 1851 as part of the Great Exhibition in London, which drew more than seventy-five thousand visitors. Among them was Queen Victoria, who later wrote in her journal, "It is impossible to imagine anything so lovely as these little Humming Birds."

This exhibit sparked a craze for hummingbirds in Europe—as an item of decoration and trade. "Their minute size and gemlike appearance caused them to be coveted as jewelry and adornment for women's hats," writes Alexander F. Skutch in his book *The Life of the Hummingbird*. He reports that a single dealer in London, over the course of a year, purchased more than four hundred thousand hummingbird skins.

It wasn't until the early 1900s that organizations such as the Audubon Society and the Royal Society for the Protection of Birds shifted the focus on hummingbirds from consumption to conservation, promoting an ethos of appreciation and protection of these unique and flamboyant creatures in the wild.

Territory

There are more than 340 hummingbird species categorized into 123 genera. Most live in the equatorial belt—a 10-degree-wide strip of territory that lies on either side of the equator—with the highest number of species found in Columbia and Ecuador. Population numbers decrease as you go north and south from that region.

Fifteen hummingbird species annually migrate to or live in the United States and Canada, and a few more have been known to visit occasionally. For those with the longest migration routes, this can mean a journey of nearly 4,000 miles (6,437 km).

The migratory pattern of West Coast hummingbirds forms a circuit—up the coast in spring, then south through the mountains toward the end of summer. This

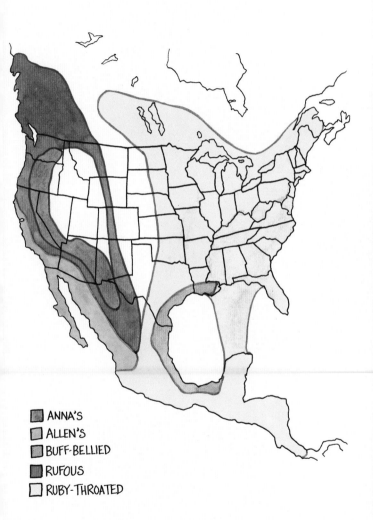

ANNA'S
ALLEN'S
BUFF-BELLIED
RUFOUS
RUBY-THROATED

Some hummingbird species take advantage of a late summer lupine bloom in the mountains.

allows them to follow bloom time, as the higher-altitude flowers blossom later in the season when the mountains have warmed up. Their tropical wintering grounds provide hummingbirds with flowers and nectar throughout the winter.

Most migratory species are found in the western states and the Southwest, with only a single species—the Ruby-throated hummingbird—that nests east of the Great Plains.

Habitat

Hummingbird habitat is far-flung and varied—they can be found from Alaska all the way down to Tierra Del Fuego, at the southern tip of Argentina and Chile, with the majority of them living in South and Central America. Hummingbirds inhabit mountain meadows, temperate woodlands, tropical rainforests, cloud forests, and deserts—living at altitudes that range from sea level to more than 16,000 feet (4,877 m) elevation in the Andes. The one unifying characteristic in these locations is a steady supply of food. Hummingbirds have a high metabolism and need to feed frequently, so an abundance of flowers is required. For this, most hummingbirds travel.

Migratory hummingbirds fly north at the beginning of spring. Males leave first, trying to arrive early enough to scout out and claim the best territory, then the females follow.

It seems inconceivable that such a small, delicate bird could withstand both the long migration and cold temperatures found in some of their habitat locations, but hummingbirds have specific adaptations to help them cope. Though they have few feathers compared to other birds, their bodies are capable of falling into a temporary hibernation, which slows down their metabolic rate and allows them to conserve energy. Their body temperature drops as much as 50 degrees, while their heartbeat can slow from 500 beats a minute to less than 50. This is how hummingbirds survive cold nights.

Life Cycle

Hummingbirds live solitary lives. Because they consume nectar, it does not behoove them to live in pairs or families—this would only introduce more competition for flowers and food. They defend their territory fiercely and do not form lasting bonds with mates or offspring.

Most hummingbird species have a lifespan of 4 to 6 years. There are examples, however, of birds who have lived much longer. A Broad-tailed hummingbird captured in Colorado was tagged, released, and recaptured 12 years later.

Hummingbirds will begin mating after their first year. In most cases, the male stakes out territory and females come to visit. Upon a female entering his territory, a male will attempt to woo her through a courtship display of diving and shuttling back and forth—showing off his flight prowess. If the female is impressed, she will turn toward him. If not, she will fly away. After mating, the male does not participate in nest building, incubating, or feeding the newly hatched young. One male may mate with multiple females in a breeding season, and females may have multiple mates as well. As hummingbird expert Lanny Chambers reports, "These are *not* romantic birds."

After mating, female hummingbirds build a nest (though a few species start nest construction beforehand). Padded with bits of plant fiber and thistle or dandelion down, the nest is bound with spiderweb silk and decorated with pieces of moss or lichens to provide camouflage and protection from predators.

A hummingbird clutch typically consists of two eggs, each about the size of a small jelly bean and weighing no more than a gram. The eggs are white, occasionally speckled, and are laid one at a time, often a day or two apart. The incubation period is approximately 2 weeks (slightly more or less, depending on species); females take only brief breaks from incubating their eggs to feed nearby.

Hummingbird chicks, or hatchlings, emerge with almost no feathers. They are pink- or gray-skinned and weigh less than a dime. The mother hummingbird feeds her chicks a high-protein diet of insects to promote fast growth and strong bones and beaks, and nectar to help meet their energy needs. Most species feed their young for the first month of life.

At about 2 weeks, hummingbird chicks begin to test their wings in preparation for flying, which takes place within the first month. Hummingbirds prepare to leave the nest—called fledging—soon after. Though this process takes longer for some species in tropical climates, the birds quickly become independent and migratory species are ready to fly south.

Young hummingbirds have a high mortality rate—more than half will not reach maturity. This can be due to lack of adequate food, predator attack, or nest failure. Hummingbird predators include praying mantises, dragonflies, spiders, snakes, lizards, and frogs. Other birds, such as jays, owls, kestrels, some hawks, and merlins will also prey on hummingbirds. Small mammals can

Broad-tailed hummingbird, male (l) and female (r).

also present danger—including cats, rats, squirrels, and foxes. If hummingbird chicks are able to reach maturity, their life expectancy improves significantly.

Hummingbird Nests

Few people are lucky enough to see a hummingbird nest—they are small, well camouflaged, and often located so high on a tree they look like a branch knot or bump. The nests are briefly used; most hummingbird young will fledge within a month.

The nests themselves are tiny—some the size of a large thimble or a walnut shell (depending on species). They are built entirely by the female, who stomps on the base to create a firm platform. Some species, like Anna's hummingbird, start with the base and build the nest up while incubating her eggs, but most are completed before the eggs are laid. Nests are made to expand—with pliable walls that stretch as hummingbird chicks grow.

Nests are made of plant fibers, twigs, leaves, thistle, or dandelion down. Other sought-after material includes the soft fluff of bulrush or cattails (*Typha*), and catkins from trees like cottonwood, willow, poplar, witch hazel, maple, and alder. This is all bound using silk stolen from spiderwebs.

The nest exterior is equally entrancing, decorated with a collection of lichen, moss, and bark. This creates a mosaic that allows the nest to blend into the surrounding landscape, looking very much like the branch it is affixed to.

While most hummingbird nests are located in a tree or thick bush, some species are known for unusual placement. Nests have been found on the top of laundry lines, in hanging flower baskets, on a porch light, or on a water sprinkler head. Some hummingbirds build on top of the nests of other species, or reuse what they can from an older nest site. Calliope hummingbirds are known for building their nests on top of a conifer cone.

As female hummingbirds can raise multiple broods in one mating season, she may build a new nest near the first one. She may even lay her second clutch of eggs in the new nest before her first brood has fully fledged.

Nesting cycle of a hummingbird.

How a Hummingbird Works

Small but speedy. Tiny but
aggressive. Little bodies, big
appetites. Hummingbirds
are a study in extremes.

—KIRSTEN SCHRADER

Hummingbirds are marvels of evolution and natural engineering, with numerous adaptations to allow them to fly far and fast. Everything from the nature of their beak to the functionality of their tongue—and the lack of functionality of their feet—serves to maximize flight potential. This is how they manage feats of physical strength like flying across the Gulf of Mexico, as the Ruby-throated hummingbird does each spring. It's no surprise that so many have developed an admiration and affection for these tiny birds.

Wings and Feathers

Like their closest avian relative the swifts, hummingbirds stroke their wings both up and down (most birds exert power only on the downstroke). This gives hummingbirds far greater maneuverability. They can hover, fly backward, forward, and even upside down for brief periods. Hummingbird flight speeds approach 30 mph (48 kph) and can go up to 70 mph (113 kph) while diving.

Their agility comes from the way their wings move—in rapid figure-eight patterns, with 180-degree range of motion. This allows hummingbirds to hover for sustained periods and helps them feed from flowers when there isn't a conveniently located branch to perch on. Even

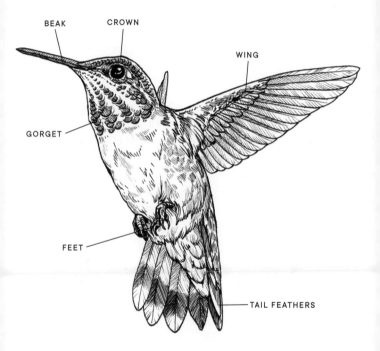

BEAK

CROWN

WING

GORGET

FEET

TAIL FEATHERS

when visiting feeders that have a built-in perch ledge or bar, many hummingbirds will choose to hover instead.

Their wingbeats are strong and rapid—up to 90 beats per second in some smaller species, and more than 200 beats per second while diving. This is the reason hummingbird wings in motion look like a blur.

That blur is often a colorful one, as hummingbirds flaunt shades of turquoise, cobalt, magenta, purple, and more. Like many birds, the female of the species is less colorful than the male—many in gray, green, and brown. Colors come from pigments inside the feathers. Some feathers can change color—flashing from dark to brilliant. This is because hummingbird feathers are iridescent.

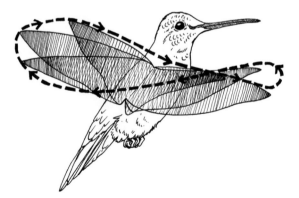

When in flight, each hummingbird wing makes a figure-eight motion.

This iridescence is caused by what is called structural coloration, which either reflects, scatters, or absorbs different wavelengths of light. It is structural coloration that makes a butterfly's wing shimmer, a soap bubble look like a rainbow, and the elaborate tail feathers of a peacock seem to glow. Hummingbirds also see color and iridescence differently than humans (more on this on page 35), so it's hard to imagine how colorful the hummingbird's world must look.

Heart

Proportionally, hummingbirds have one of the largest hearts of all animals—a full 2.5 percent of their body weight (for comparison: the human heart is only 0.3 percent of body weight). Hummingbirds need that capacity to power their wings. While in flight, a hummingbird heart may beat 1,260 times per minute (a pigeon in flight beats only 600 times per minute). Hummingbirds can also calm down their heart rate to 50 beats per minutes when they enter hibernation mode (see Torpor, page 37).

Tongue and Beak

For years it was thought that hummingbirds sucked the nectar from flowers through their very long beak using a process called capillary action that wicks liquid upward. Modern video technology now shows that it is a curling motion of the tongue that draws the nectar up so it can be consumed.

The hummingbird's tongue, which is forked at the end, is lined with hairlike extensions called lamellae. These hairs extend and then roll inward to trap the nectar as the tongue is withdrawn. It's not a terribly effective method of extraction, as not much nectar is trapped with each pull. The key is to do it over and over again: a hummingbird tongue can lap up nectar thirteen times in one second!

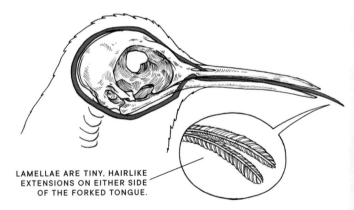

LAMELLAE ARE TINY, HAIRLIKE
EXTENSIONS ON EITHER SIDE
OF THE FORKED TONGUE.

A hummingbird tongue retracts into the bird's head and coils around its skull.

Hummingbirds have long beaks in relation to their bodies. Some have evolved in tandem with certain flowers so their beaks fit perfectly to access nectar. It's a win-win relationship; hummingbirds need the calories the flowers offer and the flowers depend on the pollination services the birds provide. The pollen a hummingbird picks up from one flower is transferred to other flowers the bird visits, this helps the plant set and produce seeds for the next season.

Eyes

Hummingbird vision is unparalleled, and for good reason. To maneuver as quickly as they do, their eyesight must be top-notch. Hummingbird eyes have both binocular vision (to look ahead) and monocular vision (to see objects on either side and in the periphery). If anything poses a danger, a hummingbird can react quickly and flit away.

Hummingbirds also see ultraviolet light, unlike humans. Their eyes have a fourth color cone that extends the range of their vision. Hummingbirds are able to perceive colors we don't even know exist.

This color perception is all in service of being able to locate the flowers that will provide the nectar they need to survive and thrive. It's common knowledge that hummingbirds favor red flowers—a reason that hummingbird feeders are usually red. There are also many stories of gardeners and other outdoor enthusiasts who have had hummingbirds attracted to a particularly colorful hat or shirt they've worn.

Another important hummingbird adaptation is a nictitating membrane, or third eyelid. Regular eyelids block light, but a nictitating membrane—commonly found in fish, amphibians, reptiles, and birds—is clear. In the case of hummingbirds, this eyelid functions like goggles and protects them while flying at high speeds.

Feet

Hummingbirds—along with their relatives the swifts—belong to the order of birds called Apodiformes. Translated from the Latin, this means "footless" or "without feet."

While hummingbirds do have feet, they aren't very functional—used mostly for perching and scratching. Their legs are also quite short, an adaptation to reduce weight and make them more aerodynamic.

Hummingbirds cannot walk or hop like most birds can. When collecting materials to build a nest, a female hummingbird will carry plant fiber or lichen in her beak rather than in her claws. The feet are necessary, for hummingbirds must take breaks between their high-energy flying, but beyond perching on a branch or twig to rest, they don't get much use.

Torpor

Hummingbirds go fast, but they can also slow down their systems, reducing body temperature and metabolism to a sleeplike state called torpor that is similar to hibernation. They do this when temperatures drop or when food conditions require it—if they cannot get enough calories to maintain their metabolism, they turn it down.

Hummingbirds enter torpor any time they cannot maintain their usual body temperature of above 100 degrees F (38 degrees C). Their feathers do not provide much insulation, so rather than expending extra energy to stay warm, they go into semi-hibernation. Hummingbirds in colder climates use this energy-saving technique to get through cold nights. When the weather warms up, hummingbirds speed up their system again.

Food Sources

Hummingbirds are sugar junkies—consuming about half their body weight in sugar every day. The flower nectar they seek is about 26 percent sugar—double what is found in a soda. (Scientists are studying the hummingbird's ability to consume that much sugar without falling into a diabetic coma.) Due to their flight habits, hummingbirds have high energy needs and that sugar is quickly burned off. They eat frequently—as much as every 10 minutes—to replenish their energy stores.

But not even hummingbirds can live on sugar alone. They also consume insects for protein and minerals—feeding on ants, aphids, fruit flies, gnats, weevils, beetles, mites, mosquitoes, and more. They either glean these insects off leaves and trees or pluck them out of the air with their beak (called hawking). They also steal insects that have become tangled in spiderwebs. In one day, a hummingbird can consume more than a thousand insects.

Still, nectar makes up an essential part of the hummingbird's diet, providing the calories needed for them to fly as they do. Hummingbirds are so protective of their nectar sources they've been known to fight other birds to defend a particularly good stand of blooms.

Hummingbirds also seek out the sap wells made by other birds drilling into trees and will feed off the sap that flows. If the sugars in the sap have attracted insects, the hummingbird may be able to fulfill multiple nutritional needs at once.

Selected Species

Included here are hummingbirds regularly found in the United States and Canada, as well as a few visiting species that spend most of their time in other locations.

A group of hummingbirds is sometimes referred to as a hover, a bouquet, a shimmer, or even a tune.

—MELISSA GISH

A male Allen's hummingbird on a willow branch.

Allen's Hummingbird

Selasphorus sasin

LENGTH: 3.5 in (9 cm)

WEIGHT: 0.1–0.14 oz (2.8–4 g)

WINGSPAN: 4.3 in (11 cm)

The January return of the Allen's hummingbird to the California coast, just as winter rains begin to coax blooms from early flowers, is one of the first signs of spring. Nesting in a narrow strip of territory that stretches up the shoreline into southern Oregon, the male Allen's prefers open scrub and chaparral, while the female makes her nest in the thickets and coastal forest.

They may be a sign of spring, but Allen's are dressed in autumn hues—the male with bronze-green upperparts, a brilliant coppery-orange throat patch or gorget, and cinnamon-colored flanks. Females lack the gorget but have a whitish throat with bronze spotting. Allen's resemble the Rufous hummingbird and the two occasionally hybridize in areas where their breeding territory overlaps. The male Rufous has a rusty-colored back, while Allen's males are green. Female and juvenile Allen's and Rufous look so similar they cannot be easily distinguished in the field.

There are two subspecies of Allen's hummingbirds. *Sasin* migrates south from the California and Oregon coasts to central Mexico each winter, while *sedentarius* is a year-round resident of Southern California, breeding in and around the Channel Islands off the coast of Los Angeles. Due to the mild climate and their resident status, *sedentarius* are able to hatch up to four broods in a year.

Allen's are fierce defenders of their territory, known for their dramatic flight displays. The male swings back and forth like a pendulum, making a trilling, cricket-like sound at the high point on either side, before ascending up to 100 feet (30 m) and plummeting in a power dive. The male pulls out of the dive just above the target of his display, making a loud metallic shriek with his feathers. This maneuver is used to woo a mate and also to drive off intruders in his territory. Of all the North American hummingbirds, it is considered one of the most impressive flight displays.

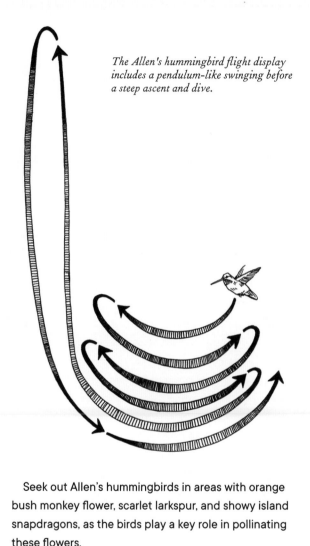

The Allen's hummingbird flight display includes a pendulum-like swinging before a steep ascent and dive.

Seek out Allen's hummingbirds in areas with orange bush monkey flower, scarlet larkspur, and showy island snapdragons, as the birds play a key role in pollinating these flowers.

Anna's Hummingbird

Calypte anna

LENGTH: 3.9 in (10 cm)

WEIGHT: 0.1–0.2 oz (2.8–5.7 g)

WINGSPAN: 4.7 in (12 cm)

That flash of magenta you see in the garden might just be an Anna's hummingbird, the most common species along the Pacific Coast. Traditionally their territory was limited to Baja and Southern California, but thanks to a wider planting of exotic trees and flowers in backyard gardens, as well as hummingbird feeders, Anna's can now be found as far north as Alaska and British Columbia, and east into New Mexico. They've even been known to breed with other hummingbird species: Allen's and Costa's.

Male birds are easy to spot—their crown and throat flashes a dazzling hot pink when sunlight hits it. Juvenile males and females have metallic green coloring with streaks of gray. Anna's tend to be a stocky species, about the size of a golf ball. They serve an important role as pollinators in their traditional breeding grounds, the chaparral coastlands of California.

In their courtship display, the Anna's male ascends to a height of 130 feet (40 m), then dives toward the female. At the bottom of the dive, a squeaking noise can be heard. For years this sound was thought to be part of their birdsong repertoire, but analysis of high-speed video has shown that the squeak is caused by air passing over their outer tail feathers.

Anna's hummingbirds do sing—a series of crackly buzzes, chirps, and whistles. If his courtship dive has been successful, a male will follow the female toward her nest performing a shuttle display, swinging back and forth, often singing.

Unlike some species, Anna's hummingbird population numbers have steadily increased since the 1950s, at a rate of about 2 percent a year. This is thanks, in part, to the introduction of eucalyptus trees to the West Coast in the mid-nineteenth century, which provided Anna's with a favored habitat and food source.

Anna's hummingbird female (l) and male (r) on manzanita branches.

Black-chinned Hummingbird

Archilochus alexandri

LENGTH: 3.5 in (9 cm)

WEIGHT: 0.1–0.2 oz (2.8–5.7 g)

WINGSPAN: 4.3 in (11 cm)

Darting through the garden with great speed and agility, the male Black-chinned hummingbird shows off a stripe of iridescent purple like a necklace below his dark-colored head and white spots at the outside corner of his eyes. Their bodies are long and slender, with a long black bill and whitish underparts with some light brown mottling below the wings.

The female and young male have no such adornment—nor black chin. Instead they feature brown speckling over the crown and upperparts of metallic green; they also have the white spot on the outer corners of their eyes.

Black-chinned hummingbirds have a breeding range that stretches from the southern part of British Columbia in the north, through Idaho, Nevada, and all the way down to northern Mexico, with a swath that runs from the coast of California east into Texas. They winter in the southern portions of California, Arizona, Texas, and in Mexico.

Known to be quite adaptable to their environment, Black-chinned hummingbirds can be seen in urban and suburban areas, as well as deserts and forests, so long as there are adequate flowering shrubs and vines, and tall trees to nest in.

Black-chinned hummingbird courtship rituals include a pendulum display, where the male attempts to impress a female by diving back and forth in a U-shaped arc while making a whirring sound that repeats with each dive.

Black-chinned and Ruby-throated hummingbirds look quite similar, but they inhabit very different territory. Black-chinned hummingbirds are found exclusively in the western states, while the nesting territory for the Ruby-throated is east of the Great Plains.

The oldest known Black-chinned hummingbird was found in Texas in 2008—a banded female who was recaptured 11 years and 2 months after being registered.

Black-chinned hummingbird male (l) and female (r) feed on columbine nectar.

Blue-throated Mountain-gem Hummingbird

Lampornis clemenciae

LENGTH: **4.3–5.5 in (11–14 cm)**

WEIGHT: **0.27 oz (7.6 g)**

WINGSPAN: **3 in (7.6 cm)**

The largest of all hummingbirds in the United States is the Blue-throated mountain-gem—a visitor from Mexico who nests in the wooded mountain canyons of southern Texas and Arizona. At three times the size of a Ruby-throated hummingbird, Blue-throated mountain-gems are the dominant hummingbird species in their territory. They have even been known to drive off larger birds of prey—such as northern goshawks—and sometimes work cooperatively to do so.

With a cerulean blue gorget, bronzy-green upper-parts, and soft gray underparts, the male has a striking appearance. Females have crowns of the same bronzy-green color, though no gorget. Both males and females sport a jaunty white streak coming off each eye like a racing stripe.

The Blue-throated mountain-gem is known for its birdsong. Males often sing from high tree perches, especially in the morning, and sometimes vocalize with other males in adjoining territory. Females are also known to sing and occasionally duet with male suitors during courtship.

Spring arrivals begin in March in the "sky island" mountains of southern Arizona and the Chisos region of Texas. Blue-throated mountain-gems breed and nest near flowing water, in shady sycamore, oak, and pine forests. Their breeding season runs from April to October and may include up to three broods.

Blue-throated mountain-gems have three subspecies: *bessophilus* and *phasmorus* can be found in the southern United States, while the largest subspecies, *clemenciae*, is found only in Mexico.

*Blue-throated Mountain-gem hummingbird male (l)
and female (r) seek out lobelia blooms.*

Broad-billed Hummingbird

Cynanthus latirostris

LENGTH: 3.25–4 in (8.25–10.2 cm)

WEIGHT: 0.1–0.13 in (2.8–3.7 g)

WINGSPAN: 5 in (12.7 cm)

The Broad-billed hummingbird wears the colors of a tropical ocean—emerald, teal, and turquoise. The male has a deep, purply-blue gorget and a red bill tipped in black. The female is less flamboyant: mostly pale gray with hints of green and a dark-colored bill, but distinctive for a white stripe that begins just behind the eye.

Both males and females have tails that are notched in the middle, though female tails have rather squared corners, while male tails are thicker and have rounded corners.

Female and juvenile Broad-billed hummingbirds can easily be confused with White-eared hummingbirds, though the color of their ear patches differ. The Broad-billed ear patches are gray; the White-eared blackish.

Found mostly in western Mexico, the Broad-billed territory reaches up into the southernmost parts of Arizona and New Mexico, where the birds can be seen in the mountainous canyons, usually below 2,000 feet (610 m), nesting in trees along streambeds. When annual rains cause the wildflowers at higher altitudes to bloom, they forage the mountain meadows up to nearly 10,000 feet (3,048 m) in elevation.

While other hummingbird species favor a dramatic dive pattern in their courting rituals, the Broad-billed hovers and swings back and forth like a hypnotic pendulum. After mating, the female builds a nest quite low to the ground—starting at about 3 feet high. Unlike other hummingbird nests, they are not decorated with lichen.

Favored nectar sources include bird-of-paradise, coral bean, fireweed, paintbrush, and penstemon, as well as desert willow and several types of agave and honeysuckle. Look for Broad-billed hummingbirds in areas with Fremont cottonwood, honey mesquite, Arizona white oak and sycamore, red barberry, soap-berry, and wooly buckthorn.

Broad-billed hummingbird male (l) and female (r) on coral bean flowers.

A male Broad-tailed hummingbird and scarlet gilia.

Broad-tailed Hummingbird

Selasphorus platycercus

LENGTH: 4–4.5 in (10–11.4 cm)

WEIGHT: 0.11–0.14 oz (3.1–4 g)

WINGSPAN: 5 in (12.7 cm)

If you hear an oddly metallic trilling sound while in a wildflower meadow in the mountains of Colorado, you might be in the presence of the Broad-tailed humming-bird, whose males make the sound by beating their wings. Males flaunt a dazzling magenta-pink throat and metallic green upperparts. Females share the same upperparts but underparts are speckled with brown, green, and bronze. A white eye-ring is an identifying characteristic, as is the broad, rounded black tail from which they get their name.

With territory that stretches from Guatemala and Mexico in the south, to Montana in the north (a few visitors have even been sighted in Canada), Broad-tailed hummingbirds can be found in the subalpine zone—ranging from mountain wildflower meadows to pinyon-juniper woodlands and ponderosa pine forests, at elevations from 5,000 to 10,500 feet (1,524–3,200 m). In the winter they forage in the Mexican highlands, seeking out pine-oak and dry thorn forests.

They are drawn to brightly colored flowers with high sugar content—paintbrush, sage, scarlet gilia, larkspur, and red columbine.

Broad-tailed hummingbirds breed and migrate at higher altitude, where nighttime temperatures can drop significantly. Because of this, they make use of hypothermic torpor—dropping their body temperature and slowing their heart rate to save energy. Females often build their nests under overhanging branches, which—along with the insulating qualities of the nesting materials—helps keeps them warmer at night.

The Broad-tailed hummingbirds are experiencing a slow and gradual decline with a loss in population of almost 50 percent since the 1960s. While the full cause is not clear, climate change is likely a contributing factor. Severe winters have impacted their numbers, and when wildflower bloom at breeding sites occurs earlier than usual, it limits the time when nectar is available to the birds. Some of these changes may be offset by the growing popularity, at least in populated areas, of hummingbird feeders to supplement nectar sources.

Broad-tailed hummingbird preening.

A male Buff-bellied hummingbird perches on an anacua branch.

Buff-bellied Hummingbird

Amazilia yucatanensis

LENGTH: 3.9–4.3 in (10–11 cm)

WEIGHT: 0.14–0.18 oz (4–5 g)

WINGSPAN: 5.75 in (14.6 cm)

With territory that hugs the Gulf of Mexico, from Guatemala and Belize in the south up through coastal Mexico and southern Texas, Buff-bellied hummingbirds are a rare species with members that migrate *north* in the winter—into coastal Louisiana, Mississippi, Alabama, and even northern Florida. However, their breeding grounds are mostly in southern Texas, and they can be reliably sighted there from April to August. Look for Buff-bellied hummingbirds at bird feeders in park visitors' centers in the area.

Known for their relative size—larger than most of the hummingbird species seen in the United States and Canada—and their sometimes-aggressive behavior, Buff-bellied hummingbirds flaunt an iridescent blue-green throat and breast. As their name suggests, their belly is a buff or beige color, with charcoal gray wings and a bill of bright red with a black tip. Tail feathers flash a pale cinnamon-rust color.

There are three subspecies, identified by their underparts—*chalconota*, found in Texas, has the lightest colored belly. *Yucatanensis* and *cerviniventris* have cinnamon-colored and darker brown bellies, respectively. Buff-bellied hummingbirds are also known for their vocalization, which includes several distinctive sounds. There is a *tsi-we* or *siik* that is used during display flights; a repetitive dry *tuk*; and *see-see-see-see-su-su*, employed while chasing other hummingbirds away.

Due to their size, Buff-bellied hummingbirds can be pugnacious—quick to drive off a Ruby-throated or Black-chinned hummingbird from an appealing flower or bird feeder. Though chasing is common, no physical contact has been observed.

Buff-bellied hummingbirds are found in shrubby and woodland habitats, and in suburban parks and gardens as well. They are frequently sighted in the lower Rio

Grande Valley of Texas, where they prefer to roost in the understory of hackberry, pecan, anacahuita, papaya, ash, and Texas ebony trees. Favored nectar sources include tropical sage, Turk's-cap lily, coral bean, aloe vera, anacua, and mesquite plants.

The female Buff-bellied hummingbird seeks out the nectar of coral bean flowers.

A male Calliope hummingbird feeds on larkspur nectar.

Calliope Hummingbird

Selasphorus calliope

LENGTH: 3.1–3.5 in (8–9 cm)

WEIGHT: 0.1 oz (2.8 g)

WINGSPAN: 4.1–4.3 in (10.5–11 cm)

The Calliope hummingbird is the smallest long-distance migratory bird in the world, traveling more than 5,000 miles (8,046 km) from winter grounds in southern Mexico to breed in the mountain meadows of the western United States and Canada. These tiny birds are often chased by other, more aggressive hummingbirds—such as the Rufous, with whom they share breeding grounds. As a result, the Calliope keeps a low profile, foraging and perching close to the ground.

The male Calliope has a distinctive gorget of dazzling magenta in a starburst pattern below his bill. The female and juvenile Calliope share the same iridescent green upperparts and crown as the male, but their breast is buff colored and lightly speckled. Though they resemble Broad-tailed and Allen's hummingbirds, they are significantly smaller.

In courtship, the male performs a dive-and-shuttle flight display that produces a high-pitched zing-like call. While shuttling, the feathers of his gorget flare to look like a flower, and the male hovers with a wing speed so rapid—42 percent higher than normal—that it sounds like a bumblebee.

If a female Calliope responds to a male's courtship display, she joins him in a aerial dance, and they circle and spin together, occasionally clasping each other's bill. A male Calliope may mate with numerous females during breeding season, which lasts from April to June.

Calliope nests are usually built in conifer trees: lodgepole pine, Douglas fir, or western red cedar. They are sometimes built on the base of a pinecone, or on top of the remains of a nest from prior years.

Calliope hummingbirds breed in the mountains and meadows of the West—in Northern California, Nevada, Utah, Oregon, Washington, Idaho, Montana, and into western Canada. Their migrations take them from the rainforests of southern Mexico through grasslands, scrub forests, deserts, and even into tundra. They are most likely to be found at higher elevation, from 2,645 to 7,495 feet (806–2,284 m).

*Calliope hummingbirds prefer to build their
nests in the boughs of conifer trees.*

Costa's Hummingbird

Calypte costae

LENGTH: 3–3.5 in (7.6–9 cm)

WEIGHT: 0.11–0.12 oz (3.1–3.4 g)

WINGSPAN: 4.3 in (11 cm)

A desert dweller, the small Costa's hummingbird pro-
vides a flash of dazzling purple in an arid landscape.
They are found in the Sonoran and Mojave deserts in
Arizona, Nevada, Southern California, and down into
Mexico and the Baja peninsula, where Costa's also live
year-round in the coastal scrub.

While the female Costa's is fairly nondescript, with
green over whitish underparts and a thin black bill, the
male more than makes up for it with a flamboyant crown
and purple gorget that glows iridescent magenta in the
sunlight. A male Costa's gorget extends to either side
(called a gorget flared), giving him the look of a masked

bandit. When wooing, the male will hover in front of the female, looking like a brilliant mask or large appealing flower (some have said it resembles a baby octopus).

Female and juvenile male Costa's are sometimes confused with female or young Anna's or Black-chinned hummingbirds. Anna's tend to be slightly larger and the throat patch—present in almost half of female Costa's—is more purple for Costa's, redder for Anna's. Female Black-chinned hummingbirds have a longer bill and no throat patch.

March and April are the months to catch Costa's hummingbirds in the desert areas of Arizona and California, where they breed before the summer temperatures rise. Year-round populations can be found in the chaparral and sage scrub of coastal Southern California.

Costa's are chatty birds, with both the male and female making regular vocalizations. The male gives a high, thin whistle during breeding seasons, including during an elaborate dive and whistle display that has the male Costa's looping around and over the female repeatedly. The female also calls frequently.

While Costa's hummingbirds visit a variety of desert flowers in search of nectar, they favor chuparosa and ocotillo. In California, they can be found feeding on bush monkey flower, white and black sage, and heart-leaf penstemon, among others.

Costa's hummingbird female (l) and male (r) on ocotillo.

Lucifer Hummingbird

Calothorax lucifer

LENGTH: 3.5 in (9 cm)

WEIGHT: 0.1–0.11 oz (2.8–3.1 g)

WINGSPAN: 4 in (10.2 cm)

Most frequently found on Mexico's arid central plateau, the Lucifer hummingbird crosses the US border to nest and breed in the Chihuahuan Desert of west Texas, southern Arizona, and New Mexico from March to September, then retreats to Mexico for the winter.

This small hummingbird sports a distinctive down-curved bill. Both males and females have green backs, though the male stands out with a striking purple gorget—a common name used for the birds in nineteenth-century Mexico was *Morado Grande*, or Big Purple—while females have buff-colored breasts flanked by cinnamon. The Lucifer belongs to the sheartail group of hummingbird species, who all share a narrow tail with a deep center fork.

Lucifers are known to favor penstemon, trumpet flower, cholla, anisacanth, and especially agave—where they act as nectar thieves. Agaves have evolved to be pollinated by the longnose bat. The petite hummingbirds are much smaller than the bat, they are able to feed without disturbing the pollen—thereby getting a free lunch without providing any services in exchange. When it comes to ocotillo flowers, however, Lucifers may lose out on the nectar. Local carpenter bees are the thieves in that situation, piercing the base of the flowers to get to the nectar first.

Lucifer hummingbirds are also notable for mating displays at the nesting site of the female. While she is nest building—a process that can take up to 2 weeks—the male performs a 6-foot shuttle maneuver, back and forth, before ascending up to 100 feet (30 m) and diving down. When performing the shuttle portion of the mating display, the Lucifer hummingbird makes a noise similar to a deck of cards being shuffled. This is the only known nest-side courtship, and the display may be repeated up to five times in an hour.

Lucifer hummingbird male (l) and female (r) perching on tree cholla.

Rivoli's Hummingbird

Eugenes fulgens

LENGTH: 4.3–5.12 in (11–13 cm)

WEIGHT: 0.26–0.30 oz (7.4–8.5 g)

WINGSPAN: 7.1 in (18 cm)

Rivoli's was once called the Magnificent hummingbird—and the name is apt. One of the most striking of the hummingbirds north of Mexico, Rivoli's is named after French nobleman and amateur ornithologist Victor Masséna, the third Duke of Rivoli, whose large collection of bird specimens can be seen today in the Academy of Natural Sciences at Drexel University in Philadelphia. (Anna's hummingbird is named after Masséna's wife.)

In 2017, scientists divided the Magnificent hummingbird into two species, calling the northern species (which breeds in Mexico and the southern United States) Rivoli's, the original name given to them in 1829.

The southern species was renamed Talamanca, after a mountain range in Costa Rica where they are found.

At 5 inches long, Rivoli's is the second largest hummingbird to nest in the United States (Blue-throated mountain-gems are the largest). With territory that stretches as far south as Nicaragua, Rivoli's can be found in southern Arizona and a bit of western New Mexico during the breeding season from April to early October.

The male Rivoli's is an eye-catcher, with a brilliant purple crown, iridescent green gorget, and black underparts—unusual among North American hummingbirds. Out of direct sunlight they can look dark, then flare into color when light hits their feathers. Females lack the brightly colored head and breast and have lighter underparts—a dappled gray pattern with green upperparts. Both male and female have a dark-colored bill and a small white smudge behind each eye.

Rivoli's hummingbirds can be found in dry pine-oak forests and along canyon bottoms. Look for them in Arizona alder and cypress, Douglas fir, pinyon, and juniper. Rivoli nests are built high—10 to 60 feet (3–18 m) above the ground. While there is little research on Rivoli's preferred nectar sources, contenders include paintbrush, red columbine, Jacob's ladder, penstemon, and giant trumpet vine.

Rivoli's hummingbird male (l) and female (r) feed off of agave nectar.

Ruby-throated Hummingbird

Archilochus colubris

LENGTH: 3–3.5 in (7.6–9 cm)

WEIGHT: 0.11–0.12 oz (3.1–3.4 g)

WINGSPAN: 3–4 in (7.6–10.2 cm)

For many, the Ruby-throated hummingbird is *the* hummingbird of summer—the only species regularly found
east of the Great Plains. They have the largest breeding
range in North America, from central Canada to the Gulf
of Mexico. In the winter, they retreat to Mexico, Costa
Rica, and Panama, many of them migrating across the
Gulf of Mexico, a journey of 500 miles (805 km).

This migration is one of the fascinating things about
Ruby-throated hummingbirds. Under normal circum-
stances, hummingbirds must feed regularly, due to the
tremendous amount of energy they burn. But those who
cross the gulf do so in a single flight, flying low over the

water without stopping or resting. To accomplish this, they feed heavily before the journey, nearly doubling their body weight.

Spring migration starts as early as February, with the males departing first. The returning fall journey begins in August. Not all undertake the cross-gulf flight, however. A number of Ruby-throated hummingbirds fly around the gulf, making the coast of Texas a hotbed for hummingbird sightings during migration season.

Ruby-throated hummingbirds live up to their name, with the male sporting a dark gorget that turns brilliantly flame-colored in sunlight. The male also has a dark crown and mask, mottled light underparts, and metallic green and gray back and wings. The female is less flamboyant, with light underparts and a metallic green-gray back.

Ruby-throated hummingbirds can be found in the mixed woodlands and deciduous forest in the eastern United States and up into southern Canada. They favor the edges of woodlands, gardens, and parks. Their arrival is not timed to the blooming of particular flowers, but it takes place after the arrival of the yellow-bellied sapsucker—in order to assure a food source in case of the absence of flowers. Ruby-throated hummingbirds feed at sapsucker wells in birch, tulip poplar, and red maple trees.

*Ruby-throated hummingbird female (l) and male (r)
sample the nectar of spotted jewelweed flowers.*

Rufous Hummingbird

Selasphorus rufus

LENGTH: 3.5 in (9–10 cm)

WEIGHT: 0.11–0.16 oz (3–4.5 g)

WINGSPAN: 4.5 in (11.4 cm)

Rufous are the long-distance travelers of the hummingbird world—migrating from central Mexico to Alaska, a one-way journey of roughly 4,000 miles (6,276 km). The migration route is an oval circuit—running up the California coast in the early spring to the Pacific Northwest, then down an inland Rocky Mountain route to take advantage of high-altitude wildflowers in the late summer and early fall.

Rufous is both a name and a description of the rusty color of this tiny hummingbird. Males have a copper-colored gorget, as bright as a new penny, with a white collar below the gorget and ruddy-brown feathers on both upper and underparts. Females lack the bright rusty-colors, sporting metallic green and gray on the back and a speckled throat with lighter underparts, but they do have some rufous tail feathers tipped in white. Both male and females have a white spot just behind each eye.

Rufous are feisty and territorial, quick to defend their claim to a hummingbird feeder or a particularly choice stand of flowers—even taking on larger species. They are partial to red columbine, scarlet gilia, salvias and mints, the early spring flowering currant (*Ribes sanguineum*), and fireweed.

Their breeding territory is large—Oregon, Washington, Idaho, western Montana, and up through British Columbia and into southern Alaska. Nests may be built in conifers—western red cedar, spruce, hemlock, Douglas fir, and pine. Colonies of up to twenty nests in close proximity have been reported in Alaska, British Columbia, and coastal Washington.

Rufous are easily mistaken for Allen's hummingbirds— the species were once classified together—and it can be difficult to tell the two apart in the wild. They have territory ranges that abut each other in southwest Oregon where hybridization is likely, making identification even more challenging.

*Rufous hummingbird female (l) and male (r) are
attracted to the nectar of red paintbrush flowers.*

A male Violet-crowned humming-bird perches on honey mesquite.

Violet-crowned Hummingbird

Leucolia violiceps

LENGTH: 4.3 in (11 cm)

WEIGHT: 0.16–0.20 oz (4.6–5.8 g)

WINGSPAN: 5.9 in (15 cm)

First recorded in the southern United States in 1959, the Violet-crowned hummingbird is essentially a Mexican species that seems to be increasing its range northward. It can now be found in southern Arizona and New Mexico in gradually increasing numbers, even overwintering in the canyons there.

With a snowy white breast, a long, orangey-red bill tipped in black, and a crown that runs iridescent violet to cobalt blue, these larger-sized hummingbirds attract attention as they perch and nest in the sycamores and cottonwoods that grow along streams and canyon creek beds of the Southwest. Males are known to sing at dawn.

Males and females look largely the same, each with bronzy-green upperparts and a spot of white behind the eyes. Juveniles have crowns of brown or bluish green, muted colors, until their adult plumage comes in. The Violet-crowned hummingbird is the only species found in the United States where the male does not have a gorget or throat patch.

Breeding in Arizona and New Mexico starts in April and extends into September. Violet-crowned hummingbirds scout locations from about 4,000 to 5,600 feet (1,219–1,706 m), though they often range into higher altitudes in search of flowers and feeders. Nests are chiefly in sycamore trees—often in open areas, but the nests themselves are shaded by a large leaf. Nearby foliage includes agaves, honey mesquite, little-leaf sumac, ocotillo, willows, velvet ash, and big-tooth maple.

In these Southwest canyons, the Violet-crowned hummingbird often shares territory with other hummingbirds—Broad-billed, Broad-tailed, Black-chinned, Rufous, and Costa's. Due to their relative size, however, Violet-crowned hummingbirds are the dominant species, chasing off smaller birds from shared nectar sources and sometimes guarding favored flowers. But Violet-crowned hummingbirds are, in turn, dominated by larger species—the Blue-throated mountain-gems and Rivoli's.

There are two subspecies of the Violet-crowned hummingbirds. The *ellioti* have a darker turquoise in their crown and green notes in their tail feathers. They are found in the Southwest and down to Michoacán, Mexico. The *violiceps*, whose crown is more violet and tail feathers more copper, are found from Michoacán south to Oaxaca.

A Violet-crowned hummingbird feeding her young.

A male White-eared hummingbird and parrot flower.

White-eared Hummingbird

Basilinna leucotis

LENGTH: 3.5–3.9 in (9–10 cm)

WEIGHT: 0.1–0.12 oz (2.83–3.4 g)

WINGSPAN: 5.75 in (14.6 cm)

White-eared hummingbirds appear most commonly in Mexico and down through Guatemala, Honduras, El Salvador, and Nicaragua. They have been known to nest north of the Mexican border, however, and can be found as a regular—if not common—visitor in Arizona (Coronado and Gila National Forests, especially), New Mexico (Lincoln National Forest), and Texas (Big Bend National Park). Vagrants have been sighted in Colorado and as far east as Alabama.

The "white ears" refers to a white racing stripe that begins just behind the eye and runs down the neck on either side. Males have a blue-purple crown and chin with a gorget that glitters emerald green; the female's crown is dark and her throat is whitish with specks of green. Both male and female have a somewhat broad bill with a black tip and a base of orangey-red (females have more black on their bill; males have more red). Upperparts are coppery-green on both and turn rusty toward the tail. They are members of the emerald group, or clade, of hummingbird species.

White-eared hummingbirds can be found in pine-oak and Douglas fir forests, especially along the edge, and in clearings between 4,000 and 11,500 feet (1,219–3,505 m) in elevation. Look for them near their favored sources for nectar: agaves, firecracker bush, scarlet creeper, parrot flower, salvia, Mexican cardinal flower, and Turk's-cap lily. They can be found in the US borderlands during breeding season from March to October, after which they return to Mexico.

Though White-eared hummingbirds can be aggressive—known for driving off larger birds from their favored nectar sources—they nest in close proximity with each other. White-eared males also sing together as part of their mating ritual—as do several hummingbird species—in groups of up to seven members called leks. Their birdsong is a repetitive metallic chirp described as *chi-tink, chi-tink, chi-tink.*

Of the three subspecies, *borealis* is found in northern Mexico and the US borderlands; territory for *leucotis* covers central and southern Mexico and Guatemala; and *pygmaea*, the smallest of the three, is native to El Salvador, Honduras, and Nicaragua.

A female White-eared hummingbird feeds on the nectar of the firecracker bush.

Creating a Hummingbird Haven

Let a man plant a flower garden almost anywhere from Canada to Argentina and Chile . . . and before long his bright blossoms will be visited by a tiny glittering creature that hovers before them.

—ALEXANDER F. SKUTCH

One of the best ways to deepen your relationship with hummingbirds is to invite them into your garden. The delight of seeing these extraordinary creatures flit and dart at close range is ample payoff for the effort. Plus, the more support hummingbirds get, the better chance they have of thriving and multiplying.

You can encourage hummingbirds to make your territory their own by providing for their needs—planting flowers or hanging feeders for food, giving water and shelter, and minimizing the dangers they might encounter. You don't even need a garden to encourage hummingbirds—a feeder or hanging planter basket can be attached to a balcony or the eaves of a roof.

Food

Hummingbirds' favorite flowers tend to be tubular shaped and brightly colored—especially red, orange, and pink. Think about choosing plants that bloom in different seasons, so there will always be something available for the birds, especially in early spring and late autumn when flowers can otherwise be scarce.

When choosing a location, clump the same flowers together, rather than scattering them around the garden, so it's easier for hummingbirds to find and partake (imagine your garden like a buffet table—put all the desserts together). Also, think of planting in layers—with flower options at different heights, from low to high. A mix of sun and shade is best for hummingbirds, with plenty of bushy options in case they need to dart out of sight of a predator.

The flower list on page 108 is divided into annuals (will bloom for one season), perennials (will return year after year), and biennials (will take 2 years to bloom). Select a variety of heights, bloom times, and cultivars that you like—and know that selecting plants native to your climate is always a wise choice. Native plants are easier to care for and your local or migratory humming-birds know them already. You'll also want to make sure the plants you are purchasing were not grown with neonicotinoids—systemic pesticides that are taken up by the plant. Neonicotinoids can be harmful to birds, bees, and other pollinators, and they kill the insects hummingbirds need to feed on.

Note: make sure to select plants that are suited to your climate, soil conditions, and gardening zone (find your zone at Garden.org/nga/zipzone/). Situate the plants according to their needs—in full or partial sun—and place those with similar water requirements close together, to make caring for them easier.

Annuals

Flowering tobacco, jasmine tobacco (*Nicotiana spp.*)

Impatiens (*Impatiens*)

Nasturtium (*Tropaeolum spp.*)

Petunia (*Petunia spp.*)—annual in most zones; perennial in Zones 9–11

Pincushion flower (*Scabiosa spp.*)—annual and perennial cultivars exist

Spider flower (*Cleome hassleriana*)

Zinnia (*Zinnia elegans*)

Perennials

Anise hyssop (*Agastache foeniculum*)

Bee balm (*Monarda didyma*)

Bleeding heart (*Lamprocapnos spectabilis*, formerly *Dicentra spectabilis*)

Canna (*Canna x generalis*)

Cape fuchsia (*Phygelius capensis*)—late blooming

Cardinal flower (*Lobelia cardinalis*)

Catmint (*Nepeta*)

Columbine (*Aquilegia spp.*)

Crocosmia or montbretia (*Crocosmia* 'Lucifer')

Daylilies (*Hemerocallis*)

Fuchsia (*Fuschia magellanica*)

Garden phlox (*Phlox paniculata*)

Hibiscus (*Hibiscus*)

Larkspur (*Delphinium spp.*)

Lupine (*Lupinus*)—early blooming

Paintbrush (*Castilleja*)

Penstemon or beardtongue (*Penstemon digitalis*)—late blooming

Petunia (*Petunia*)—perennial only in Zones 9–11

Pincushion flower (*Scabiosa spp.*)—annual and perennial cultivars exist

Salvia (*Salvia spp.*), especially scarlet sage (*Salvia splendens*)

Sweet William (*Dianthus barbatus*)

Biennials
Foxglove (*Digitalis purpurea* and cultivars)
Hollyhock (*Alcea spp.*)

CROCOSMIA

LUPINE

ANISE HYSSOP

NASTURTIUM

LEOME

HIBISCUS

SCARLET SAGE

PETUNIA

Bird Feeders

Many hummingbird aficionados take great pleasure in watching the visitors to their backyard bird feeders, but installing one is a responsibility that should not be taken lightly. If not cleaned, feeders can become contaminated with mold and bacteria that can sicken birds. In cooler weather (under 80 degrees F/26.7 degrees C), feeders should be cleaned and refilled twice a week. Once the temperature warms up, it is recommended to empty and clean hummingbird feeders every other day (either run through a dishwasher or scrub with hot soapy water). The American Bird Conservancy recommends that feeder be soaked once a week in a solution of nine parts water to one part bleach, or four parts water to one part distilled white vinegar.

Fill hummingbird feeders with a solution of 1 cup of white sugar dissolved in 4 cups of water, brought to a boil and allowed to cool completely. Do not use brown sugar or honey, as these will ferment. And while it is true that hummingbirds like the color red, it is not necessary to add red dye to the sugar mixture; some experts believe the dye may be harmful to bird health.

Because hummingbirds are territorial, you might want to hang two feeders—otherwise, one male may stake a claim and chase away other birds. Two feeders, set at least 10 feet (3 m) apart, should eliminate that problem. Avoid direct sun or deep shade, opting for dappled light instead, and hang feeders at least 5 feet (1.5 m) from the ground, out of range of pouncing cats or other predators.

Feeders can become a favorite destination of ants and wasps, who are also attracted to the sugar water. To avoid ants, consider an "ant moat," which positions a container of water above the feeder to act as a barrier (some feeders have this as part of their design). Wasps are a different issue, but a saucer-style feeder—where the sugar water is contained in a shallow bowl, as opposed to an upside-down bottle—can help prevent opportunistic wasps. Saucer-style feeders also leak less than traditional feeders. Saucer-style feeders hold less sugar solution, so they must be cleaned and refilled more frequently, but that is better for bird hygiene as well.

While some places have year-round hummingbird residents, in most areas feeders should be taken down in the winter. For regions with mild winters, put feeders out mid-March; mid-April if your winters are cold. Feeders can be removed in mid-October for colder climates; or mid-November if your climate is mild.

Water

Hummingbirds love water. They don't drink much of it—their hydration needs are mostly met through nectar—but they need it to preen their feathers. A standard birdbath, however, is not well suited to these tiny birds. If you'd like hummingbirds to visit your birdbath, make sure the water level is shallow—only an inch or two—and rough stones are placed within the bath where they can perch.

Even better than standing water, hummingbirds enjoy a fountain, mister, or bubbler, which provides water in motion. Any water feature should be raised several feet off the ground to avoid the threat of animals like cats, who like to prey on hummingbirds. Because of predators, it is best not to encourage hummingbirds to frequent ponds or streams that may be part of your landscaping.

Shelter

In addition to food and water sources, hummingbirds need shade, shelter, and places to perch and nest. Here again, it's helpful to think in layers. Plant shrubs, trees, and vines along with your flowers. Hummingbirds do not nest in birdhouses but they appreciate the safety that layered foliage provides.

Shrubs and Vines

Abelia (*Abelia*)

Azalea (*Rhododendron spp.*)

Bougainvillea (*Bougainvillea glabra*)

Butterfly bush (*Buddleia*)—can be invasive; avoid the *davidii* species

Cardinal vine (*Ipomoea x multifida*)

Elderberry (*Sambucus spp.*)

Flowering currant (*Ribes sanguineum*)—early blooming

Lantana (*Lantana camara*)

Magnifica honeysuckle (*Lonicera sempervirens*, 'Magnifica')

Red birds in a tree or Mimbres figwort (*Scrophularia macrantha*)

Rhododendron (*Rhododendron*)

Rose of Sharon (*Hibiscus syriacus*)

Viburnum (*Viburnum spp.*)—some cultivars are early blooming

Weigela (*Weigela florida*)—some cultivars are early blooming

Trees

Trees can also provide hummingbirds with food and shelter. Make sure to choose cultivars that suit your climate and fit the space available. Some—like the 'Northern catalpa'—can grow to be quite large. Others, like the 'Mimosa', are considered messy due to their sap and seedpods. Planting a tree is a long-term relationship, so make sure your selection will make you, as well as the hummingbirds, happy.

Black locust (*Robinia pseudoacacia*)—can be invasive

Crabapple (*Malus spp.*)

Desert willow (*Chilopsis linearis*)

Eastern redbud (*Cercis canadensis*)

English hawthorn (*Crataegus laevigata*)

Eucalyptus tree (*Eucalyptus spp.*)

Horse chestnut (*Aesculus hippocastanum*)

Northern catalpa (*Catalpa speciosa*)

Persian silk tree, or 'Mimosa' (*Albizia julibrissin*)—may be invasive; considered messy

Red buckeye (*Aesculus pavia*)

Strawberry tree (*Arbutus unedo*)—late bloomer

Tulip tree (*Liriodendron tulipifera*)

Vitex (*Vitex agnus-castus*)

Whiteleaf manzanita (*Arctostaphylos viscida*)

TULIP TREE

DESERT WILLOW

Safety

Dangers to hummingbirds may be hiding in your garden—chiefly, pesticides and predators. With a little care these risks can be minimized.

Pesticides used in the garden are likely to end up in the nectar of various flowers—the hummingbird's food source. If you want to encourage birdlife in your garden, it's recommended to avoid all pesticide use—both because of nectar contamination issues, and also because pesticides are designed to wipe out the insects that hummingbirds rely on for their protein. As noted on page 107, pesticides can enter your garden already inside new plants, so be cautious about what you purchase.

Hummingbird predators range from domestic cats, who can become fixated on the birds' flitting and zooming motion, to larger birds—like sharp-shinned hawks, merlins, American kestrels, Mississippi kites, and loggerhead shrikes. Other, less expected predators include praying mantises—who like to hang out on hummingbird feeders lying in wait—snakes, lizards, and bullfrogs. Make sure your feeders and water sources are located safely away from the danger these animals and insects pose.

Bird-watching

Birds really do make us
happy. They force us to stop
and pay close attention, to
notice details more acutely.

—JULIA ZARANKIN

Mexican violetear

Bird-watching is a perennially popular hobby that has recently seen a significant increase in interest. The rise of bird-related mobile phone apps, and so many photos easily available online, has made information more accessible to a wider group of people. As a result, birding is becoming both younger and more inclusive.

There's a variety of resources available to help deepen your knowledge (see Resources, page 140), but for those just starting out, here are some tips to help you begin, as well as a few of the best places to look for hummingbirds north of the US-Mexico border.

- **Look and listen:** The basics of birding are simple—keep your eyes and ears alert. You may find it helpful to use a book or mobile phone app to identify what you see and hear. *National Geographic Complete Birds of North America* or the Merlin app, from the Cornell Lab of Ornithology, are good places to start.

- **Consider investing in binoculars:** While not essential, getting a close-up view of avian species makes birding even more engaging.

- **Get out early:** There's a joke that birding will turn you into a morning person. Birds are hungry when they wake up and are most active at dawn and in the early hours. Though it's possible to bird-watch at other times of the day, avoid the noon hour, when birds are the least active.

- **Explore:** Each new location you visit will offer a different habitat—and, as a result, varied species. Birds can be found anywhere from a wilderness setting to a city park. Look high and low, as different species nest and forage in different places.

- **Connect with others:** Engaging with other enthusiasts—either online or in person—can greatly increase your knowledge, skill, and enjoyment. There are numerous birding groups, and birders are known for sharing information. You can even help contribute by participating in bird surveys—such as the Great Backyard Bird Count put on by the National Audubon Society each February—and other information-gathering efforts.

Bandelier National Monument

15 ENTRANCE ROAD, LOS ALAMOS, NM 87544

About an hour's drive from Santa Fe, in the north-central region of New Mexico, lies the 33,000 acres of canyon and mesa country that make up Bandelier National Monument. It features petroglyphs, cliff dwellings, and masonry pueblos—all historical treasures of the twenty-three tribal nations that have called this land home, going back at least 11,000 years. The park is also host to four species of hummingbirds.

The monument is located on the Pajarito Plateau in the southern Rocky Mountains, with the Jemez Mountains on one side and the Rio Grande River on the other. Here the white pine, mixed conifer, and piñon-juniper forests provide a nesting habitat for both the Black-chinned and Broad-tailed hummingbirds. These summer residents begin to show up in April, with the males arriving first to stake out territory. Rufous hummingbirds can be seen in late summer and early fall, as they return from their summer migration, and the Calliope hummingbird makes an occasional appearance.

Bentsen-Rio Grande Valley State Park

2800 S. BENTSEN PALM DRIVE (FM 2062), MISSION, TX 78572

South Texas boasts some of the most diverse bird-watching in the United States and the Bentsen-Rio Grande Valley State Park is a prime site, with 797 acres of subtropical woodlands and species that are rarely seen outside of Mexico, and nowhere else in the United States.

Centuries of river flooding from the Rio Grande has built up rich soils that support riparian woodlands studded with cedar, elm, sugar hackberry, Texas ebony, and anacua trees and host some 366 bird species, including ten types of hummingbirds.

The species found at Bentsen-Rio Grande includes: the Mexican violetear, Lucifer, Ruby-throated, Black-chinned, Anna's, Allen's, Rufous, Calliope, Broad-billed, and Buff-bellied—though not all species are regularly sighted. Most common are Ruby-throated in spring and fall, Rufous in winter, and Black-chinned all year long.

The park features the World Birding Center headquarters. There are guided tours, a two-story, extended observation platform, a birding wall, and several enclosed bird blinds to help birders get up close and personal with avian residents.

Cabrillo National Monument

1800 CABRILLO MEMORIAL DRIVE, SAN DIEGO, CA 92106

Located on the tip of Point Loma, which curves around the San Diego Bay, Cabrillo National Monument is known as the premiere bird-watching site in San Diego. Situated along the Pacific Flyway, the route for migrant avian species traveling north from Mexico and beyond, the area serves as resting stop for many bird species, including five different hummingbirds. The monument is easily accessible and even hosts a free bird-watching walk each weekend.

The species that can be seen at Cabrillo are Anna's, Allen's, Black-chinned, Calliope, Costa's, and Rufous hummingbirds. Anna's is the most numerous species in the park, while Costa's has much lower numbers. Allen's and Rufous are migrants in the San Diego area, coming through on their way north starting in February and extending to late April.

Black-chinned and Calliope hummingbirds are much rarer at Cabrillo and cause great excitement among bird-watchers, who keep a sharp eye out during the birds' migratory season in April.

Ramsey Canyon Preserve

27 E. RAMSEY CANYON ROAD, HEREFORD, AZ 85615

This preserve in the Huachuca Mountains of south-eastern Arizona offers the richest hummingbird viewing opportunity available in the United States. Located at the junction of the Sierra Madre and the Rocky Mountains, the 380-acre preserve offers a lush riparian woodland of maples, sycamores, cottonwoods, and ash, and provides critical nesting habitat for resident and migratory birds. Rising from the Sonoran and Chihuahuan deserts, the Huachuca Mountains serve as "sky islands"—their elevation presents a wide diversity of plant and animal life. The preserve hosts 170 different avian species alone.

An average year at Ramsey Canyon Preserve sees twelve hummingbird species—Anna's, Berylline, Black-chinned, Blue-throated, Broad-billed, Broad-tailed, Costa's, Lucifer, Rivoli's, Rufous, Violet-crowned, and White-eared. These hummingbirds are migratory and all return to Mexico for the winter months. The preserve is administered by the Nature Conservancy, which features a live hummingbird camera feed on its website. The viewing season runs from late March through September.

Allen's hummingbird hatchlings.

Glossary

APODIFORMES: an order of birds, comprised of swifts and hummingbirds, that features long, narrow wings and weak feet.

CROWN: the top portion of a head.

FLEDGLING: a young bird that has recently acquired flight feathers.

GLEANING: a feeding strategy by which birds pluck prey (mainly arthropods) from foliage, the ground, or other surfaces.

GORGET: a patch of color on the throat of a bird or other animal; from the French *gorge*, meaning throat.

HATCHLING: a young animal that has recently emerged from its egg.

HAWKING: the method by which hummingbirds snatch insects in midflight.

HOVER: to remain in one place in the air.

IRIDESCENT: luminous colors that seem to change depending on angle and light.

METABOLIC RATE: the amount of energy used by a body within a certain amount of time.

NECTAR: a water-based solution of sugars, such as fructose, glucose, and sucrose excreted by plant blossoms.

NESTLING: a young bird not yet ready to leave the nest.

PERCH: to stand or rest on an object or elevated location.

PREEN: for a bird to straighten and clean feathers with its beak.

Broad-tailed hummingbird preening.

RUFOUS: a rusty, reddish-brown color.

TORPOR: a state, similar to hibernation, in which an animal slows its metabolic functions to conserve energy.

TROCHILIDAE: the biological family in which hummingbirds are classified.

ULTRAVIOLET: the light waves beyond violet on the color spectrum; these waves are not visible to the human eye.

UNDERPARTS: the belly, undertail, chest, flanks, and foreneck of a bird.

UPPERPARTS: the back, rump, hindneck, and crown of a bird.

VAGRANT: a bird that is outside its wintering or breeding grounds.

Resources

There is a worldwide community of avid birders and hummingbird enthusiasts as well as numerous organizations that support continuing education. Here are a few resources to get you started.

Websites

American Bird
Conservancy
ABCBirds.org

American Birding
Association
Aba.org

American Ornithology
Society
AmericanOrnithology.org

Avibase
Avibase.bsc-eoc.org

eBird—The Cornell Lab of
Ornithology
Birds.Cornell.edu/home

National Audubon Society
Audubon.org

National Geographic
NationalGeographic.com

Books

A Field Guide to Hummingbirds of North America, by Sheri L. Williamson (Houghton Mifflin, 2001).

Hummingbirds, by Ronald Orenstein, photography by Michael and Patricia Fogden (Firefly Books, 2018).

Hummingbirds: A Celebration of Nature's Most Dazzling Creatures, by Ben Sonder (Courage Books, 1999).

Hummingbirds: A Life-size Guide to Every Species, by Michael Fogden, Marianne Taylor, and Sheri L. Williamson (Ivy Press, 2016).

The Hummingbird Handbook: Everything You Need to Know about These Fascinating Birds, by John Shewey (Timber Press, 2021).

Hummingbirds Checklist

Visit SasquatchBooks.com/wp-content/uploads/2023/09/Hummingbird-checklist.pdf to download a checklist to track your sightings of the hummingbird species that appear in this book.

Lupine "Manhattan Lights"

TARA AUSTEN WEAVER is an award-winning writer and editor. She is the author of several books, including *Orchard House*, a finalist for the 2016 Washington State Book Awards, *Growing Berries and Fruit Trees in the Pacific Northwest*, and the Little Book of Flowers series: *Peonies*, *Dahlias*, and *Tulips*. Tara writes frequently about gardening, agriculture, food, art, travel, social justice, and the environment. More information can be found at TaraWeaver.com.

EMILY POOLE was born and raised in the mountain town of Jackson Hole, Wyoming. After receiving her BFA in illustration from the Rhode Island School of Design, she returned west to put down roots in the mossy hills of Oregon. She can be found exploring tide pools and cliffsides, gathering inspiration, and making artwork about our fellow species and how to be better neighbors to them.

Printed in China

SASQUATCH BOOKS with colophon is a registered trademark of Penguin Random House LLC

28 27 26 25 24   9 8 7 6 5 4 3 2 1

Text: Tara Austen Weaver | Illustrations: Emily Poole
Editor: Hannah Elnan | Production editor: Peggy Gannon
Designer: Anna Goldstein

Library of Congress Cataloging-in-Publication Data

Names: Weaver, Tara Austen, author. | Poole, Emily, illustrator.
Title: A little book of hummingbirds / Tara Austen Weaver ; illustrations
   by Emily Poole.
Description: Seattle : Sasquatch Books, [2024] | Series: Little book of
   natural wonders
Identifiers: LCCN 2023013349 | ISBN 9781632174987 (hardcover)
Subjects: LCSH: Hummingbirds. | Hummingbirds–Pictorial works.
Classification: LCC QL696.A558 W43 2024 | DDC 598.7/64–dc23/
   eng/20230516
LC record available at https://lccn.loc.gov/2023013349

ISBN: 978-1-63217-498-7

Sasquatch Books | 1325 Fourth Avenue Suite 1025 | Seattle, WA 98101

SasquatchBooks.com

MIX
Paper | Supporting responsible forestry
FSC® C008047
FSC
www.fsc.org